T0063895

Micro
MONSTERS

FIRST EDITION
Editor Sheila Hanly; **Art Editor** Jill Plank; **Senior Editor** Linda Esposito;
Senior Art Editor Diane Thistlethwaite; **US Editor** Regina Kahney; **Cover Designer** Margherita Gianni;
Production Melanie Dowland; **Picture Researcher** Cynthia Frazer; **Illustrator** Peter Dennis;
Natural History Consultant Theresa Greenaway; **Reading Consultant** Linda Gambrell, PhD

THIS EDITION
Editorial Management by Oriel Square
Produced for DK by WonderLab Group LLC
Jennifer Emmett, Erica Green, Kate Hale, *Founders*

Editors Grace Hill Smith, Libby Romero, Michaela Weglinski;
Photography Editors Kelley Miller, Annette Kiesow, Nicole DiMella; **Managing Editor** Rachel Houghton;
Designers Project Design Company; **Researcher** Michelle Harris; **Copy Editor** Lori Merritt;
Indexer Connie Binder; **Proofreader** Larry Shea; **Reading Specialist** Dr. Jennifer Albro;
Curriculum Specialist Elaine Larson

Published in the United States by DK Publishing
1745 Broadway, 20th Floor, New York, NY 10019

Copyright © 2023 Dorling Kindersley Limited
DK, a Division of Penguin Random House LLC
23 24 25 26 10 9 8 7 6 5 4 3 2 1
001-333927-June/2023

A catalog record for this book
is available from the Library of Congress.
HC ISBN: 978-0-7440-7262-4
PB ISBN: 978-0-7440-7263-1

DK books are available at special discounts when purchased in bulk for sales promotions, premiums,
fundraising, or educational use. For details, contact: DK Publishing Special Markets,
1745 Broadway, 20th Floor, New York, NY 10019
SpecialSales@dk.com

Printed and bound in China

The publisher would like to thank the following for their kind permission to reproduce their images:
a=above; c=center; b=below; l=left; r=right; t=top; b/g=background

Alamy Stock Photo: ALIMDI.NET / Matthias Lenke 3clb, 3crb, 16br, 16-17cb, 17cb; **Dreamstime.com:** Asmfoto 44-45tc,
Chernetskaya 11tr, Dgilder 31crb, Iofoto 17tr, Lensonfocus 20tl, Lopolo 15tr, Marcomayer 8cra, Maumyhata 12cla;
Getty Images: Photodisc / Alastair Macewen 8tl, Stone / John Downer 24cla; **Getty Images / iStock:** The Image Bank /
Oxford Scientific 16c, 40tl; **Science Photo Library:** Wim Van Egmond 39cla, 39clb, 39bl, K. H. KJELDSEN 21tr, VW PICS /
Edwin Remsberg 24tl; **Shutterstock.com:** Agus Arsenio 18clb, LightField Studios 42bc

Cover images: *Front:* **Shutterstock.com:** 3Dstock c, thanmano; *Back:* **Shutterstock.com:** Macrovector cra, Kazakova Maryia cla;
Spine: **Shutterstock.com:** 3Dstock

All other images © Dorling Kindersley
For more information see: www.dkimages.com

For the curious
www.dk.com

Micro MONSTERS

Christopher Maynard

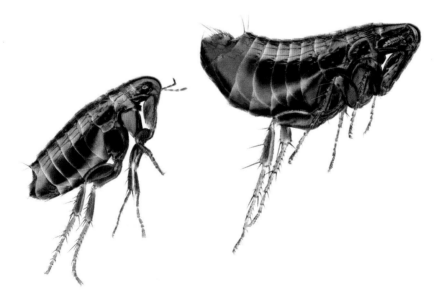

CONTENTS

Mite Fright
Some scientists think that about 90 percent of adult humans have tiny mites living at the base of their eyelashes.

IT'S A BUG'S WORLD

Meet Christopher Maynard. He is our host and the author of this book. He provides us with warmth, food, and shelter. We depend on him to stay alive, and to tell you, the reader, all about us.

Who are we? Most of us are so tiny you would need a microscope to see us properly. We are the army of tiny creatures that live on, around, and even inside Christopher's body.

Christopher is feeling awful. That's because thousands of us streptococci bacteria are growing in his throat. You can read about us on *pages 42–45*.

I am a head louse, sucking blood from Christopher's head. Read about me on *pages 8-15*.

We find shelter in his hair, feast on his skin, and tunnel into his body. And there are billions more of us who don't live on Christopher …

In the pages of this book you will see lots of close-up photographs of the tiny creatures that live on you and in the world around you. You can read all about us—in our own words.

Countless
Your body contains about 100,000 billion bacteria. But don't bother trying to count them—they are too small to see.

I am one of more than a million dust mites living in this quilt, eating Christopher's dead skin flakes. Read about me on *pages 28–33*.

I am a flea. I've just bitten Christopher's dog. Read about me and my family on *pages 16–23*.

LICE STORY

I am a common head louse. We head lice live in one place and one place only. On a human head. We can't survive on pets or birds or other animals. Only on humans.

I am about the size of a sesame seed and brownish-red in color. I have six strong, curved legs at the front of my body, which I use to cling tightly to hair. I don't have any wings, so I can't fly, but I can scurry along very fast when I need to.

Sesame seeds on bun

I spend most of my time hidden well out of sight, clinging to the bottom of a hair shaft, where it is dark and warm. The best kind of home for me is long hair, where I can hide most easily. A bald head is like a desert to a head louse.

The louse's six strong legs help it to hold tightly onto human hair.

When I feel hungry, all I have to do is crawl down the hair shaft to the scalp. It's a little like you raiding the refrigerator for a snack. I push out my long mouthparts and poke a tiny hole in the scalp. I spit some saliva into the hole. This makes the blood flow more freely so I can drink it easily and quickly.

Old Friends
Lice and humans go way back. Lice remains have even been found in the wrappings of ancient mummies.

Shaft of human hair

The hooked front legs are just the right size to grip a human hair.

Not Picky
Head lice like any heads of human hair, whether the hair is clean or dirty!

If I bit into your scalp, you would feel a little itchy. That's because my saliva is irritating to human skin. An itchy scalp may be a sign that my friends and I have come to live on your head.

Once I start feeding, I drink until my whole body is filled to bursting with blood. When I've finished my meal, my long mouthparts shrink back into my head. This meal is enough to keep me going for about three hours. I need to feed often. If I get stuck on a hat or a comb, I will soon starve to death.

No Kidding
Head lice are more often found on children than adults. This is simply because children are in closer contact with one another.

Lice Girls
Female head lice develop quickly. They can start to lay their tiny eggs at the age of only eight to nine days.

Big Families
A female louse has a huge family. In the two to three weeks that she lives, she lays about 100 eggs.

Tiny Tots
Nits are less than 0.039 inches (1 mm) long. That's about the size of the head of a pin.

Head lice grow up fast. By the age of eight to nine days, I was fully grown and I had met my mate. Soon after, she began to lay tiny silvery-white oval eggs in special casings called nits. Every night she would lay eight to 10 nits.

A young louse hatches out of the egg casing, or nit.

She carefully placed each nit on its own shaft of hair, right at the base near the warm scalp. Then she cemented it in place with special waterproof glue. That way, when our human host scratched his head or washed his hair, the nits would not work loose.

For over two weeks my mate kept laying eggs until she had laid about 100 eggs in all.

As the human's hair grew, the nits were slowly moved further from the scalp that was keeping them warm. They had to hatch before they got too far from the scalp, where they would die from the cold. After eight or nine days, out they came, exact copies of their parents, and able to feed and care for themselves.

Lice Mystery
On human girls, most nits are found over and behind the ears. On boys, most nits are found on top of the head.

Egg Head
If you find a nit more than half an inch (12 mm) away from your scalp, it will be empty. The louse inside will have hatched.

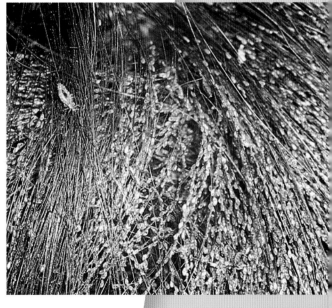

A rare case—hair with hundreds of nits

Usually no more than 10 lice live on one human head. If the head I am living on becomes too crowded, I will have to move on to another head. I can't fly or jump, so I will have to wait until another human head touches the head I am living on.

A louse scurries along a hair shaft at top speed.

Then I will run quickly along the hair shaft and climb onto the other head.

If too many of us stay on this head, our human host will start feeling very itchy. Then he might try to get rid of us. But he won't find it easy to do this. Dunking us under water makes no difference at all. Neither does shampoo or conditioner. We just hang on tightly and hold our breath.

Even anti-lice shampoo doesn't always work on us. The only thing that is certain to do the trick is patient combing with a special fine-toothed comb. It breaks our legs and loosens our tight grip on the hair. After that, it's impossible for us to hang on any longer.

Favorite Brand
If one anti-lice shampoo is used too often, lice can become immune to it— you will need to try a different brand.

The louse's mouthparts are tucked away when the louse is on the move.

A tough, leathery outer covering makes the louse hard to crush.

A nit glued onto the base of a hair shaft.

THE FLEA FILES

I am a flea. To be precise, I'm a cat flea, although right now I'm living on a dog. This isn't a problem as far as I'm concerned. We fleas live on any animal that has a permanent nest or bed, so dogs, cats, rabbits, mice, squirrels, and even humans are all good hosts for us.

Fleas and Fleas
Cat fleas have a longer snout than dog fleas have. You can see this snout only under a microscope.

A rabbit flea feeding in a rabbit's ear

Squashed Flat
Fleas' hard bodies are flattened sideways. This helps them to squeeze easily through the hair, fur, and feathers of their victims.

I've been living on my dog for several days now, ever since it went to sleep on the thick rug where I hatched out of my cocoon.

As soon as I sensed a warm body nearby I headed straight for it. I was lucky. I landed on a thick, furry coat with my first jump.

I was really hungry. So I slipped down to the skin, bit hard, and took a long drink of blood. My first warm meal made me feel better, although it didn't stop me from wanting to bite my host again. I nip him several times a minute when I'm hungry.

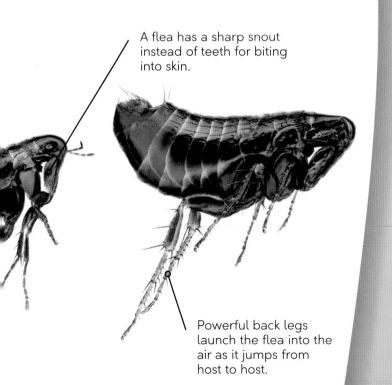

A flea has a sharp snout instead of teeth for biting into skin.

Powerful back legs launch the flea into the air as it jumps from host to host.

Big Jumpers
Fleas can jump almost 12 inches (30 cm). That's about 130 times their own size. If humans could jump 130 times their height, they could leap halfway up the Empire State Building.

Biting Back
Tiny mites live on fleas and torment them with bites, just as fleas torment us.

Bug Check
One way to check if a pet has fleas is to brush its coat over damp newspaper. If dark specks fall out and turn the paper pink, your pet has fleas—the specks are the droppings of feasting fleas.

Bloodthirsty
Like the famous vampire Count Dracula, fleas need blood to stay alive. They must drink blood before they are able to lay eggs.

In the next week or two, I'll eat about 15 times my weight in blood. Each time I feed, I'll stab the skin with my sharp snout and suck up a droplet of blood.

Our bites do not bother some hosts at all. But with hosts who are allergic, the saliva we leave in the wounds sets off an

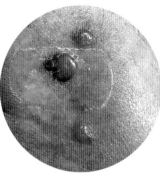

itchy skin reaction—a small spot inside a swollen red ring.

Even though two pets might be equally infested, one will scratch and nip like crazy, while the other behaves calmly as if there weren't a single flea on it.

When I'm full of blood, I don't stop to digest my meal. Instead, I keep biting my host as hard as ever. This lets me produce lots of droppings of undigested blood. These droppings fall into my host's bed, where they become food for the next generation of growing fleas.

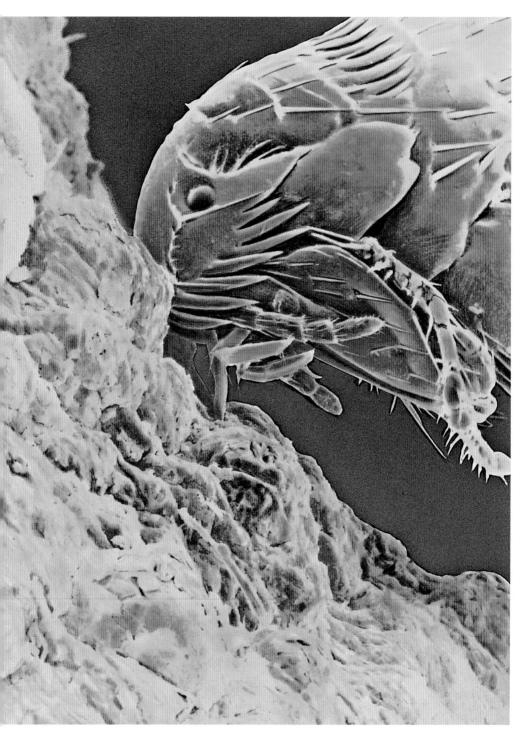

A cat flea plunging its snout into a dog's skin to suck blood

Egg Bed
Flea eggs are found anywhere their host rests—indoors in a pet's bed, or outdoors in moist sand or grit, perhaps in a pet's favorite resting place under a shrub.

I am a female flea. After mating with a male flea, I start to lay eggs. I need to be well fed and contented to do this, so I begin right after a meal. My eggs are pearly white and so small they are next to impossible to see. Usually I lay two or three a day. I place them loosely in the fur so they can drop into the place where my host is resting.

After a week or so, my eggs hatch out as little worms called larvae.

A flea larva lurking in the fibers of a carpet

How Big?
Flea eggs are small—about 0.02 inches (0.5 mm) across. You could probably fit two of them on the head of a pin. Flea larvae are a bit bigger— between 0.039 and 0.079 inches (1–2 mm) long.

Flea larvae are blind and they avoid light. They skulk in dark cracks and feed on any odd scraps they find—dead flakes of skin, hair, and the nutritious blood droppings that rain down from us feeding adults. My offspring will probably spend the whole winter as larvae before they spin silky cocoons and turn into adults as the weather gets warmer.

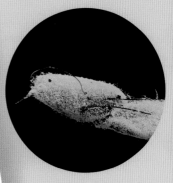

Cocoon
Flea cocoons often look like dusty balls filled with carpet fluff, hairs, and flakes of skin.

Human skin flakes

Hidden Family
Adult biting fleas make up 5 percent of fleas in a home. The rest will be eggs, larvae, or cocoons. So if you or your pets are bitten by just five fleas a day, there are probably 95 more hidden out of sight.

21

On Alert
A flea can stay in its cocoon for up to a year. But it pops out as soon as it senses the heat, vibrations, noise, or even the breath of a warm-blooded animal.

Cats and Dogs
About 95 percent of the fleas on cats and dogs in the United States are cat fleas, while pets in Europe mainly have dog fleas.

In the right conditions, our eggs can turn into adults in 10 days. It is possible for me and just nine other healthy females to have your home swarming with over 100,000 eggs, larvae, cocoons, and adults within 30 days if the weather is warm and humid.

The most likely time for us to attack is when you and your pets come back from a vacation. While you were away, all the many eggs we had laid were busy hatching out into larvae and the larvae were becoming cocoons.

The cocoons wait patiently for warm-blooded hosts to turn up. The moment a family walks in the door, every flea in the place will know about it and get set to jump aboard.

Under Attack
The worst time for humans to get bitten is when infested pets go away. Newly hatched fleas will now turn on people, although they cannot lay eggs on a diet of human blood.

House Check
One way to check for fleas is to wear white socks on a carpet that has not been walked on for several days. If more than five fleas show up on your feet and ankles, you have a serious flea problem.

23

Before feeding

After feeding

Little Vampire
A bed bug can take in six times its weight in blood at a single meal. That's like you eating about 1,600 hamburgers at a time.

Stink Bug
Bed bugs have strong scent glands. When a bed bug is frightened, it leaks an oily liquid with a disgusting, sweetish stink—some say like rotting raspberries.

NIGHT RAIDERS

I am a bed bug. I got my name because I like to live either near or in a human's bed. During the day I hide out in any dark crevice I can find—in floorboards, bed frames, alarm clocks, even the seams of a mattress.

At night, I wake up to hunt for a meal. My favorite food is human blood. I head toward the warmth of the nearest sleeping body and crawl up and down until I come across a patch of bare flesh.

Once I find a promising site I ease my sharp beak into the skin. Then, using it like a straw, I take a long drink of warm blood. To make sure my beak doesn't get blocked, I inject a drop of saliva into the hole to keep the blood flowing steadily.

I can suck for up to 12 minutes before I drop off my host as bloated as a balloon.

When I've finished my meal, I stagger to my hiding place for a few days of digesting the feast. Most humans don't feel a thing while I'm feeding on them. When my host wakes the next morning, all he notices is a hard round welt on his skin that itches like crazy where his body has reacted to my saliva.

Big Bugs
Bed bugs are only about a fifth of an inch (5 mm) long, but they are too big to fit on the head of a pin.

The bed bug uses its long feelers to "smell" the air as it searches for blood.

Bed Bug Diet
In cold places,
a bed bug can
last for 500 days
without a drop
of blood to drink.
But it would not
lay eggs in that
time.

**No Wings—
Can't Fly**
Bed bugs can't
fly. They can
only crawl.

You Look Pale
A newly
hatched bed
bug, or nymph,
is a very pale
straw color. But
it turns deep
red or purple
after its first
meal of blood.

Recently, I found myself on an empty bed. But I'm not worried. If I have to, I can wait more than six months for my next meal of blood.

In the meantime, since there is nothing to disturb me, I will lay some eggs. Usually, I produce a few dozen at a time. The eggs are covered with sticky glue that fastens them firmly to the rough surfaces of the cracks and crevices in which I place them. This keeps them from rolling away. After about two weeks, the eggs will hatch out as small, almost colorless versions of me and my mate. It will then take a couple of months for my brood to become fully grown.

If my family here ever runs out of humans, we will have to find new hosts. We bed bugs can move fast and far when we need to. We might explore along pipes to get into the homes next door, or we might hitch a ride in furniture and move to a new place altogether. We might even climb aboard passing pets or wild birds if there are no handy humans around. During the 18 months that is our life span, we can go a pretty long way in search of new hosts.

Not Fussy
If there are no human victims, bed bugs may attack guinea pigs, rabbits, rats, bats, birds, and chickens.

Bed bugs of all ages—adults, youngsters, babies, and eggs

If you collected a
quarter of an
ounce (7 g) of
house dust, there
would most likely
be over 3,000
dust mites in it.
One bed can
hold millions.

Shedding
An adult human
sheds a plateful
of skin a year—a
huge feast for
tiny dust mites!

What Size?
Dust mites
are 0.008 inches
(0.2 mm) long.
Five dust mites
could fit on the
head of a pin,
but you'd need a
microscope to
see them.

MIGHTY MITES

Did you know that more than a million eight-legged, humpbacked creatures are probably living under YOUR bed? We are dust mites—and we'll bet lots of us live all over your home. Any place that is humid and warm suits us just fine.

Mostly we live in dust, especially in places that trap tufts of it—such as deep carpets, pillows, bedding, and sofas. Dust might seem like a strange place to live. But it isn't if you look at it closely. It is mostly made up of strands of hair, clothes fibers, carpet fluff, and countless flakes of human skin. And skin flakes are what we mites really love to eat. It's why so many of us crowd together in mattresses and in carpets under beds. For us, these places are just like orchards where millions of delicious skin flakes drop from human beings every day.

We have no jaws and we can't chew our food. Instead, we belch digestive juices onto our food to turn it into liquid. Then we suck it up, just like a milkshake through a straw.

Feeling Sneezy?
Dust mites' tiny droppings fly easily into the air. When people inhale the droppings they may react by sneezing violently or even suffer an asthma attack.

The dust mite's legs end in little claws that help it grip the skin flake it is eating.

29

Mini Mites
Itch mites are 0.02 inches (0.5 mm) long. About two of them could fit onto the head of a pin.

Cross section of human skin showing a burrowing itch mite under the surface

I am a female itch mite—a cousin of the dust mites. Instead of eating skin flakes, we itch mites burrow right into human skin! The good news is that male itch mites stay on the surface and do little harm. The bad news is that we females are great diggers and can spread from person to person like wildfire.

We use our mouth and front legs to bite into skin cells and suck out the fluid inside. We don't go deeper than the outer layers of skin—that's why no blood comes gushing out—but our burrows can wind along for over an inch (2.5 cm). A burrow isn't much wider than a hair, so it's nearly impossible for humans to see. What they can't miss, though, is the itchy rash we give them.

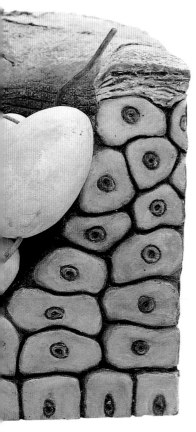

As we dig, we lay eggs, usually about three a day. After eight weeks and over 150 eggs, we die. Within three or four days the eggs hatch out and baby mites climb to the surface, where they live until they start to lay eggs themselves.

Sore and Itchy
Chemicals from the mite's body irritate the skin it digs in. This causes scabies, a disease that makes skin sore and itchy and covers it in bumps, blisters, and sores.

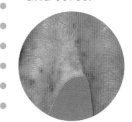

Find the Fold
Itch mites like to dig in folds of the skin at the fingers, armpits, wrists, groin, and legs.

People Carriers
Itch mites live only on humans, and scabies spreads easily. All it takes is for one infected person to shake hands with another.

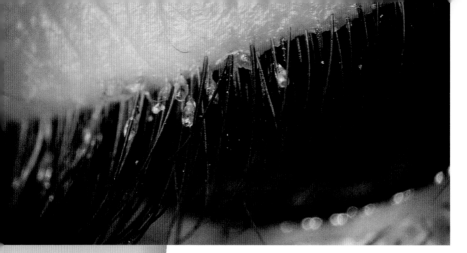

Mite Colony
Most people have colonies of eyelash mites on them and never notice a thing.

Even Smaller
An eyelash mite is about 0.003 inches (0.08 mm) long. You could fit about 12 mites on the head of a pin.

I am an eyelash mite. Imagine being as small as me and living on a great, big, blinking eyelash. Whenever the eyelids flutter, I go up and down, up and down. It's like living on a giant merry-go-round.

We eyelash mites are really small— much smaller than our itch mite cousins— and we are colorless, too. So if you haven't got a very powerful microscope, don't even try and look for us. It's impossible. But if you did look at us through a microscope you would see a hot-dog-shaped body and four pairs of legs. These are the only features that give us away.

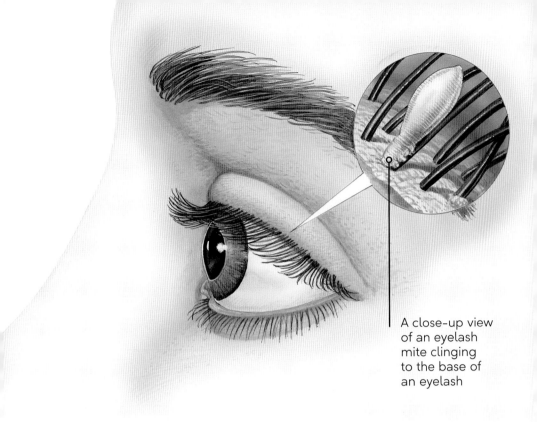

A close-up view of an eyelash mite clinging to the base of an eyelash

For most of our lives, we live harmlessly in the socket, or follicle, of an eyelash.

We hang on to the lash, always pointing head down so we can suck up the juices that ooze out of human skin. Because we don't burrow into skin, we don't have any serious ill effects on people. And because we are invisible, nobody really takes much notice of us at all.

Day and Night
Eyelash mites spend their days feeding within a hair follicle. At night they come up to the skin's surface to mate.

TALE OF A TAPEWORM

Just the One
Humans usually have just one long tapeworm at a time, although up to six have been recorded. Other animals, such as dogs, may have hundreds of short ones.

Common Worm
The most common parasite living in adult Americans is the beef tapeworm. These beef tapeworms can grow very long, with bodies made up of between 1,000 and 2,000 segments each.

I am a tapeworm bladderworm. I have just been swallowed by a human who ate the piece of meat where I was living.

At the moment, all I am is an inside-out hooked head in a casing. Once I've passed through this human's stomach and moved into the small intestine, my outer casing will dissolve and my head will turn the right side out. All my inward-facing hooks will point outward in a ring around the tip of my head. These hooks will help me attach myself to the wall of the intestine.

Once I have settled down inside my host's intestine, I will start to eat. There's so much food passing through that I will stay well fed. Though when I say "feed," I don't mean munching with mouth and teeth. I don't have any. Instead, I soak up food through my slimy skin.

Suckers keep the worm stuck in place.

Hooks sprout from the worm's head.

Monster
One of the longest tapeworms ever found inside a human was from a man who ate a raw trout. After his doctor gave him anti-worm drugs, out came a 28-foot (8.5-m) monster!

The suckers and hooks on my head are only to anchor me to the wall of the gut.

My host probably won't have a clue that I am living inside him. He might get headaches or stomach cramps. And later, if I grow very long and steal too much of his food, he may lose some weight.

Short Story
There are 3,000 kinds of tapeworm. The smallest are just 0.04 inches (1 mm) long. The biggest reach a ribbony 80 feet (24 m)— that's about as long as six cars.

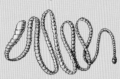

1. A human eats meat infected by a bladderworm, which develops into an adult tapeworm.

2. The adult tapeworm produces eggs, which are released in human feces.

3. The eggs are eaten by an animal and hatch into larvae.

4. Larvae enter the animal's muscles and become cysts (bladderworms).

My body is a chain of flat segments, strung together like the boxcars on a freight train. As I grow, new segments appear from my neck. Each segment is both male and female, so I can fertilize myself and produce eggs without a mate.

Once a segment of my body fills up with eggs, it drops off and passes out of my host. If these eggs are swallowed by a grazing animal, they will hatch out inside it as larvae.

Once the larvae have hatched, they will burrow through the animal's intestines and into its bloodstream. Then they will drift to other parts of its body, such as the organs and muscles. Here, they will form cysts, or new bladderworms.

If humans eat the animal's flesh without cooking it properly first, the bladderworms will turn into tapeworms inside their intestines and the cycle will begin again.

New segments are produced from behind the head.

Need a Host
Tapeworms are parasites. A parasite is an animal that can only live on or inside another animal—the host. Without a host, a parasite cannot survive.

Each segment contains both male and female sex organs.

One segment can contain about 100,000 eggs!

A tapeworm's body can be very long, but it is seldom more than 0.4 inches (1 cm) wide.

Quick Cure
A single dose of drugs will get rid of a tapeworm living inside a person's intestines.

Blob of Jelly
Amoebas have simple bodies: just an envelope of colorless jelly with a nucleus that controls how it works.

Hard Times
If food or water runs out, amoeba form a tough layer on their surface and become resting cysts. When things get better, they wake up and start to move again.

AMOEBA IN ACTION

I'm tiny—incredibly tiny. In fact, I am one of the smallest complete bundles of life possible—just a single, soft, squishy cell. Cells are the little building blocks that living beings are made of. Your body is made of billions of cells that work together to keep you alive. But I don't need other cells to keep me going. I have no head, legs, or fins, but I can move, eat, and even think for myself.

When I want to find food, I slowly slide a false foot forward.

It is called a false foot because it is actually just a branch of my body. I use my foot to probe what's out there. If it hits a bacteria, algae, or something else I can eat, I flow after it as fast as I can. Like a tiny blob of molasses, I spread out so my body completely surrounds the food particle. Then I pour in digestive juices until the food is dissolved and can be absorbed by my body.

We amoebas may be slow, but we have had hundreds of millions of years to spread around the world. I've got cousins, for example, who live only in the sea and others that live only in ponds and lakes. Some even survive as parasites in the bodies of bigger animals.

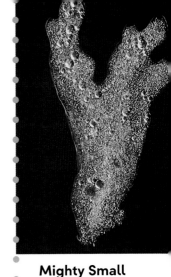

Mighty Small
This picture shows an amoeba 40 times longer than it is in real life. If you were 40 times longer, you'd probably be about twice as big as a blue whale—the largest animal in the world.

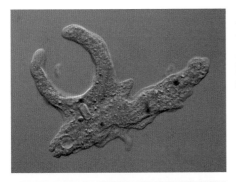

1.
The amoeba moves toward its meal and spreads its body around it.

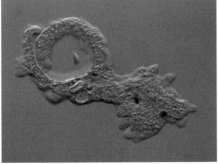

2.
The amoeba starts to encircle its prey with its body.

3.
Once it has surrounded its prey, the amoeba digests its meal.

Very Slow
An amoeba flowing along at top speed will move one inch (2.5 cm) in an hour.

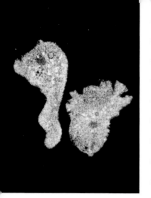

Divide and Multiply
When amoebas reproduce they simply divide into two equal (but smaller) halves. These offspring are usually called daughter amoebas.

Lots of us amoebas do no harm at all if we invade the bodies of bigger animals. A few amoebas, though, are really dangerous. They can cause illnesses such as dysentery in humans. Dysentery is a disease that sends people running to the toilet every few minutes until they get so weak they collapse. In fact, amoebic dysentery can kill if it isn't treated quickly.

This amoeba is about to surround another amoeba before eating it.

Dysentery is spread by food and water contaminated by the dysentery amoeba. This amoeba thrives wherever there are open sewers, or where raw sewage is used to fertilize crops.

When amoebas infect food and water, and then get swallowed, they make themselves at home in the human gut. The trouble starts once they invade the walls of the intestines. There they cause terrible pains and trigger bouts of dysentery. It takes several different medicines to cure the illness, although washing hands well and making sure water is pure is probably the best way to keep this disease at bay.

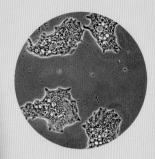

Fast Change
It takes less than an hour for a parent amoeba to turn itself into a pair of amoeba offspring.

Movie Monster
In the movie *The Blob*, filmmakers used the idea of an amoeba to create a giant blobby monster that engulfed its victims and swallowed them whole.

BILLIONS OF BACTERIA

You cough. You moan. Your throat feels raw as if a razor is cutting into it. You've caught a bug and that's where I come in.

I'm a bacteria, the smallest form of life on Earth. More exactly, I am a streptococcus bacteria (you can call me strep). I'm so small I'm invisible, but I pack a terrific wallop if I infect someone's throat. Once I get in, I multiply like crazy in the wet warmth. By the end of just one day, there may be hundreds of millions of bacteria lining the walls of the throat.

Humans react violently to me and my kin. They come down with a painful illness known as strep throat. The inside of the throat turns an angry red color.

Dot to Dot
Streptococci bacteria look like tiny dots. They clump together in chains up to 30 cells long that look like microscopic pearl necklaces.

Winter Worry
People often get strep throat in winter, but being outside in the cold is not to blame. Instead, it's being cooped up indoors that helps germs to pass back and forth on coughs and sneezes.

Streptococci bacteria growing on human tonsils

Hair-like threads help this bacteria to move around.

A slimy outer layer keeps the bacteria from drying out.

Smallest of All
Bacteria are so small that about 1,000 could fit on the head of a pin.

Not Just Strep
Only one child in 10 with a sore throat and fever can blame it on strep bacteria. The other nine children can blame it on virus infections.

It becomes dotted with specks of pus. Glands in the neck swell up and become tender. Soon swallowing hurts so badly it is almost impossible to eat. Fever, chills, headaches, and stomachaches pile on the misery. Even with medical attention, people stay sick anywhere from three to five days.

Baby Boom
While still in its mother's womb, a human baby is completely free of bacteria. But the instant babies are born, they start to acquire billions of bacteria. From then on, humans are like walking gardens of bacteria.

Billions
The human body has more bacteria than it has cells. Many cluster on the skin. Others line the mouth and nose. Still more live in the intestines, where they help to keep humans healthy.

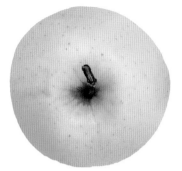

Fortunately, I am a mild bacteria. It is easy to get rid of me using antibiotics—drugs that help the human body fight off bacteria. But I have relatives who are real thugs and can do nasty things to humans.

My cousins E.coli are common bacteria that live in animal intestines. There they stop other harmful bacteria from growing and help to make important vitamins. But one rare strain of the family is a brute. It can wreck the lining of the intestine and cause terrible cramps, diarrhea, and vomiting. It is mostly picked up by people who have eaten undercooked infected meat.

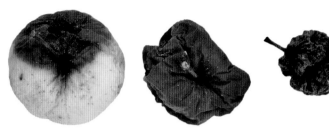

These photographs show an apple rotting. Once an apple is damaged, it is infected with bacteria that break down its cells.

Lots and Lots
There are more than 10,000 known kinds of bacteria and an unknown number more still waiting to be discovered.

But please don't get me wrong. Not all of us bacteria are bad guys. Some of us do a lot of good.

For example, soil is packed with all kinds of bacteria. Many of us spend our time recycling animal dung or making sure dead creatures and plants rot. We can help to keep a field of cows healthy by working with dung beetles to break down the cows' dung and turning it into mulch to enrich the soil.

If we bacteria didn't do our stuff, dead plants and animals would litter the landscape forever.

Simple Shapes
Bacteria belong to four main groups: the round beaded types (called cocci), short rods (called bacilli), bent rods (called vibrios), and spiral shapes (called spirilla).

GLOSSARY

Antibiotics
Drugs that stop the growth of or destroy living things that cause diseases in animals

Cells
The building blocks that make up all living things

Cocoon
The soft casing in which a larva develops into the next stage of its life

Contaminate
To infect something by touching it or mixing with it

Feces
Solid waste or droppings that pass out of animals

Follicle
The socket from which a hair grows

Glands
Structures inside a plant or animal that produce chemicals such as digestive juices

Host
A living thing on which other living things feed

Infect
To pass on or spread a disease

Infest
To swarm or attack in a troublesome way

Intestines
The tubes inside the body that digest and absorb food and water

Larva
A young animal that is completely different from an adult animal of the same kind.

Liver
An organ in the body that produces chemicals to break down fatty food

Microscope
An instrument with lenses that makes things look bigger

Nucleus
A structure inside a cell that tells the cell what to do

Nymph
A young, partly developed insect

Parasite
A living being that can only survive by living on or in another living being

Red blood cells
Blood cells that carry oxygen around the body

Vitamins
Substances that an animal needs in order for its body to grow and work well

Warm-blooded animal
Animals whose bodies stay at a constant warm temperature. All birds and mammals are warm-blooded.

INDEX

QUIZ

Answer the questions to see what you have learned. Check your answers in the key below.

1. Where do lice live?

2. When are fleas most likely to bite?

3. How long can bed bugs wait for another meal of blood?

4. What do dust mites like to eat?

5. What's the smallest form of life on Earth?

6. How does a tapeworm feed?

7. How does an amoeba find food?

8. True or False: Bacteria only cause harm.

1. On a human head 2. When people and pets come back from being away 3. Six months 4. Flakes of human skin 5. Bacteria 6. It soaks up food through its skin 7. It slides its false foot forward 8. False